The Joy of
George Gershwin

Celebrated songs, themes, and pieces of George Gershwin.
Selected and arranged by Gerald Martin.

Exclusive Distributors:
Music Sales Limited
8/9 Frith Street, London W1V 5TZ England
Music Sales Pty. Limited
120 Rothschild Street, Rosebery, Sydney, NSW 2018, Australia

ISBN: 0.7119.1384.6
Order No. YK 21442

Yorktown Music Press
London/New York/Sydney

£10.50

√ = done

x = do

I Got Plenty of Nuttin'

from Porgy and Bess (1935)

**Words & Music by George Gershwin,
DuBose & Dorothy Heyward & Ira Gershwin**

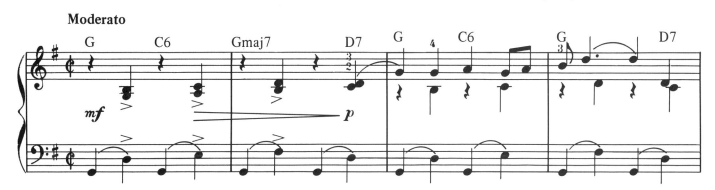

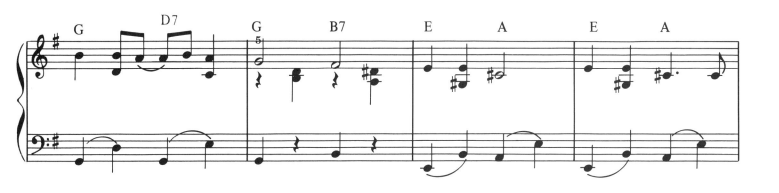

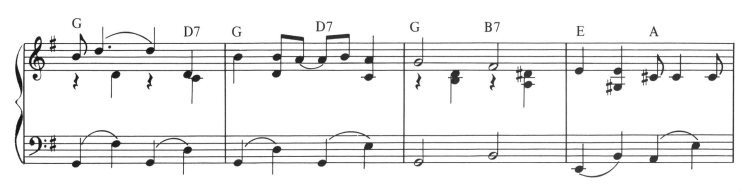

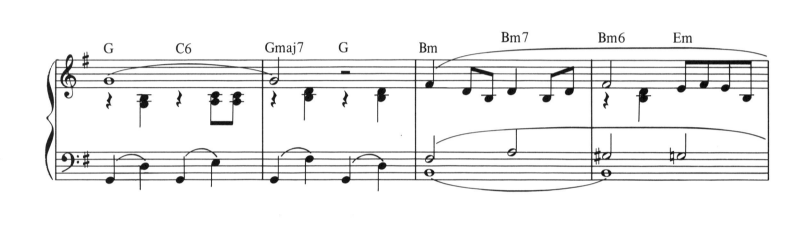

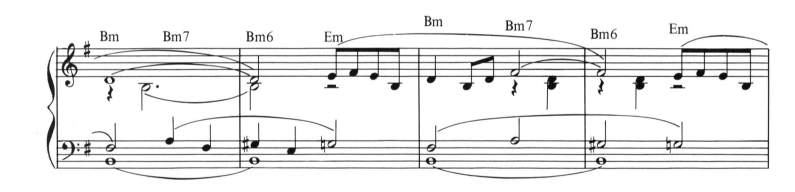

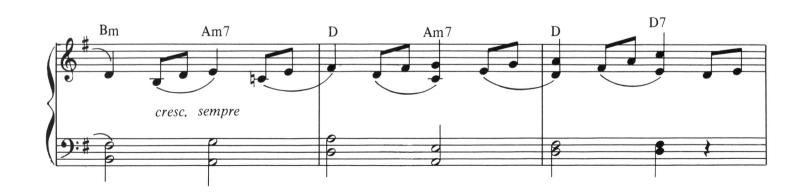

Swanee

from Capitol Revue *(1919)*

**Music & Lyrics by George Gershwin
& Irving Caesar**

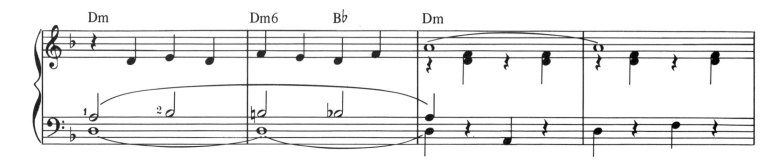

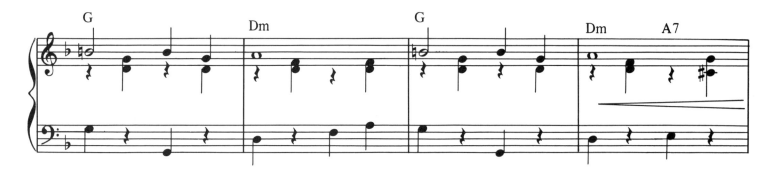

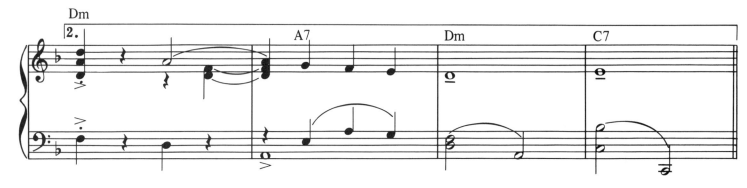

'S Wonderful

from Funny Face (1927)

Music & Lyrics by George Gershwin & Ira Gershwin

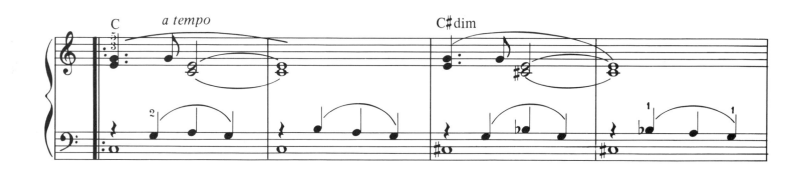

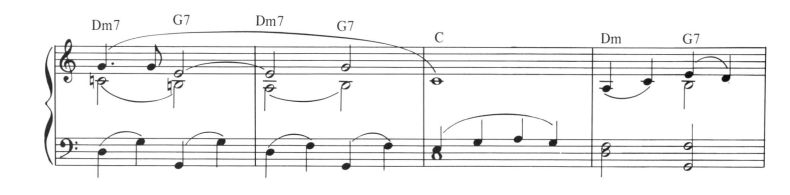

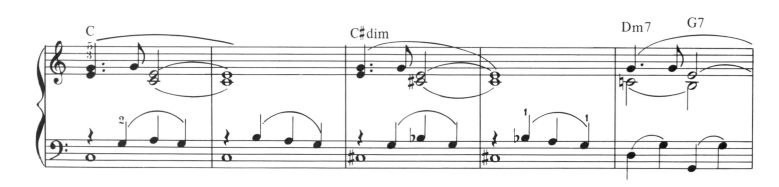

Bidin' My Time
from Girl Crazy (1930)

Music & Lyrics by George Gershwin
& Ira Gershwin

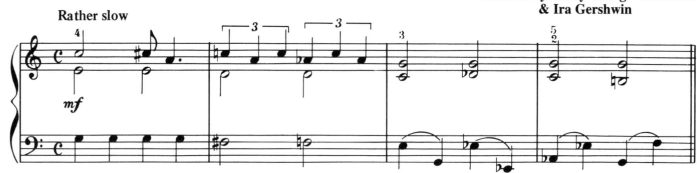

Chorus:

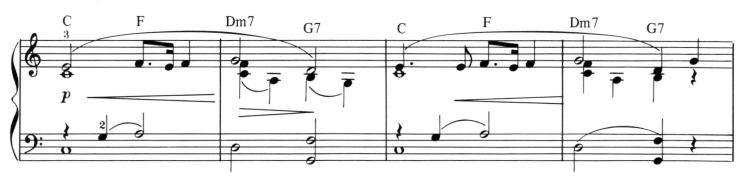

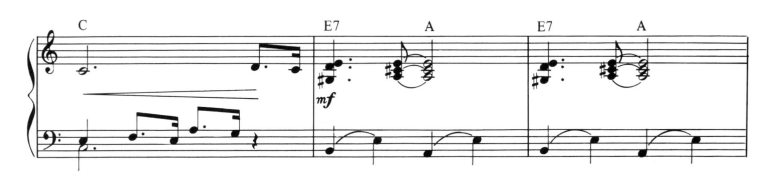

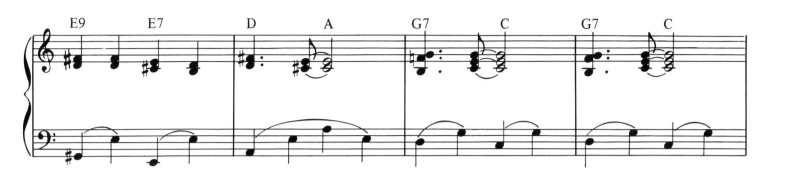

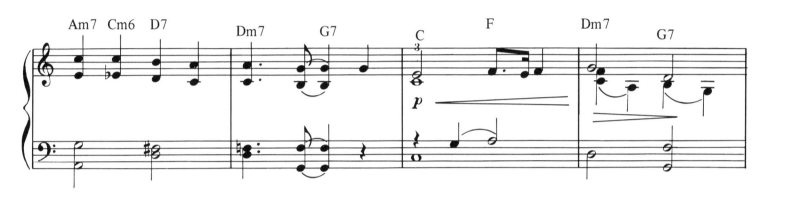

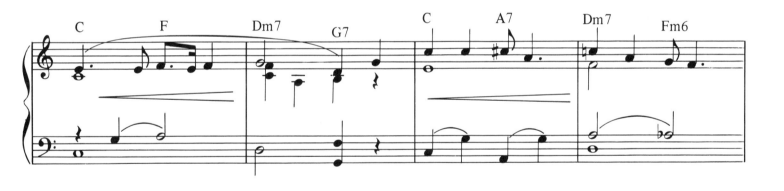

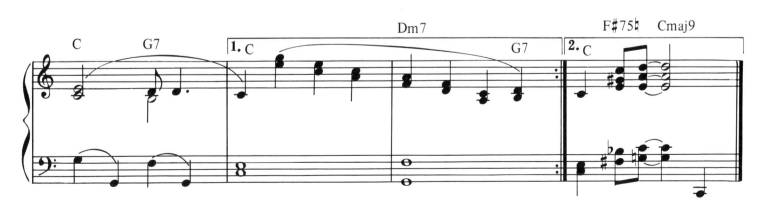

The Man I Love
from Lady, Be Good! *(1924)*

Slowly and freely

Music & Lyrics by George Gershwin
& Ira Gershwin

Embraceable You
from Girl Crazy *(1930)*

**Music & Lyrics by George Gershwin
& Ira Gershwin**

Somebody Loves Me

from George White's Scandals of 1924

**Music & Lyrics by George Gershwin,
Ballard MacDonald & B.G. DeSylva**

Of Thee I Sing

from Of Thee I Sing *(1931)*

**Music & Lyrics by George Gershwin
& Ira Gershwin**

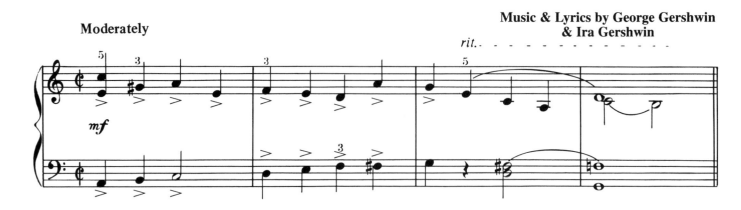

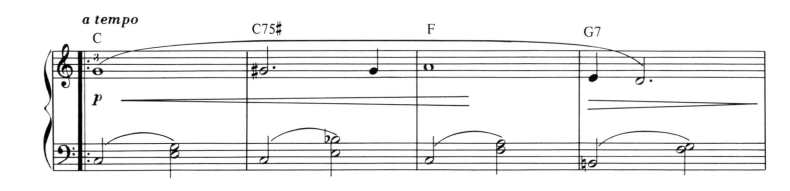

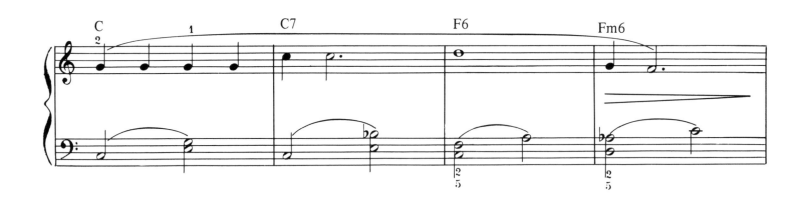

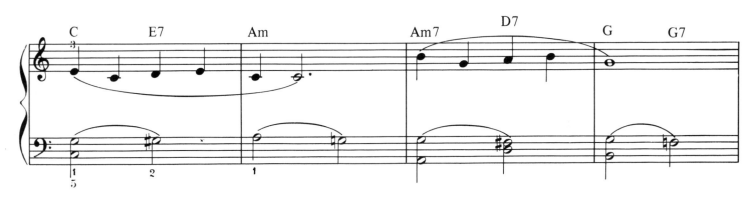

Strike Up The Band

from Strike Up The Band *(1930)*

**Music & Lyrics by George Gershwin
& Ira Gershwin**

Fascinating Rhythm
from Lady, Be Good! *(1924)*

Solid, moderate beat

Music & Lyrics by George Gershwin
& Ira Gershwin

Liza
from Show Girl (1929)

Moderate lilting tempo

Music & Lyrics by George Gershwin,
Ira Gershwin & Gus Kahn

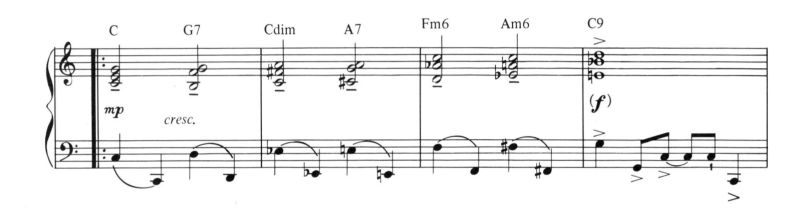

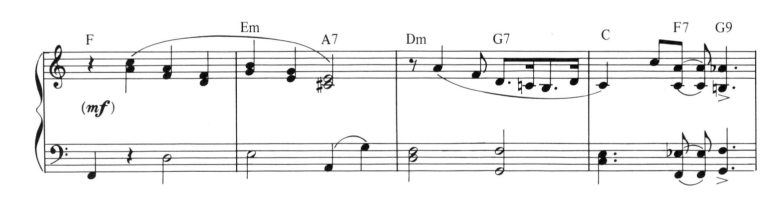

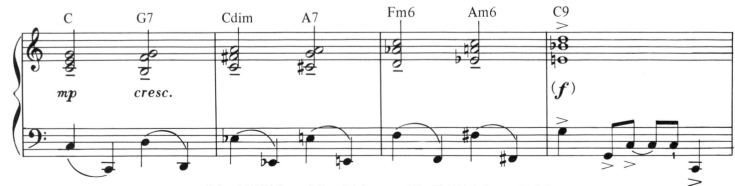

Someone To Watch Over Me

from Oh, Kay! *(1926)*

Music & Lyrics by George Gershwin
& Ira Gershwin

Oh, Lady Be Good

from Lady, Be Good! *(1924)*

Graceful walking beat

Music & Lyrics by George Gershwin
& Ira Gershwin

I Got Rhythm

from Girl Crazy *(1930)*

**Music & Lyrics by George Gershwin
& Ira Gershwin**

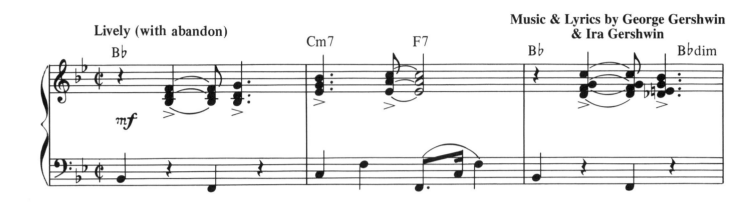

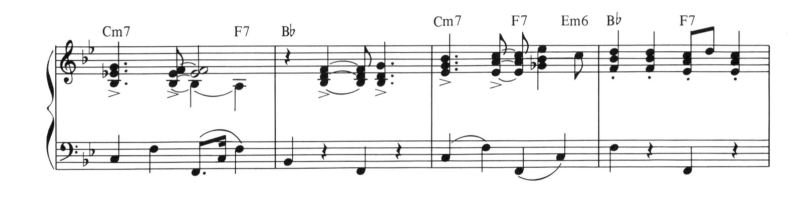

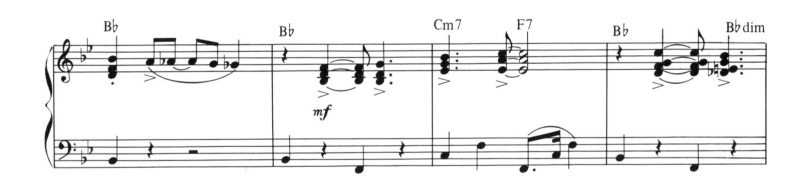

Let's Call The Whole Thing Off

from Shall We Dance *(1937)*

Music & Lyrics by George Gershwin
& Ira Gershwin

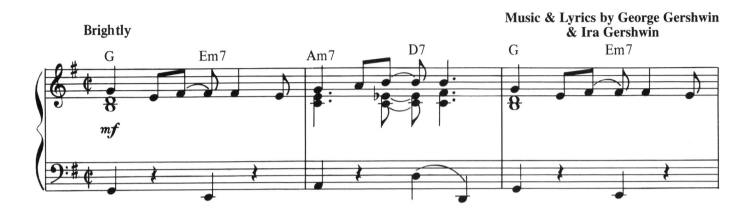

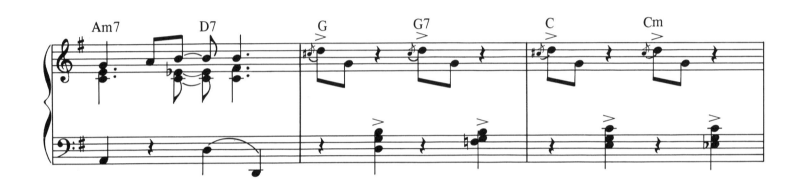

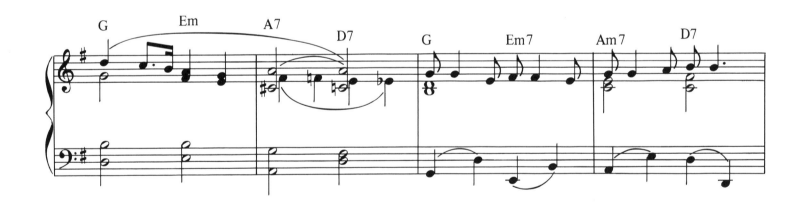

It Ain't Necessarily So

from Porgy and Bess *(1935)*

**Words & Music by George Gershwin,
DuBose & Dorothy Heyward & Ira Gershwin**

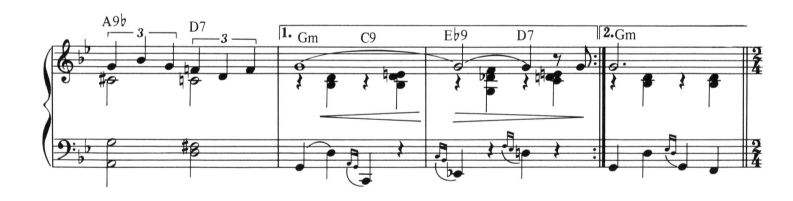

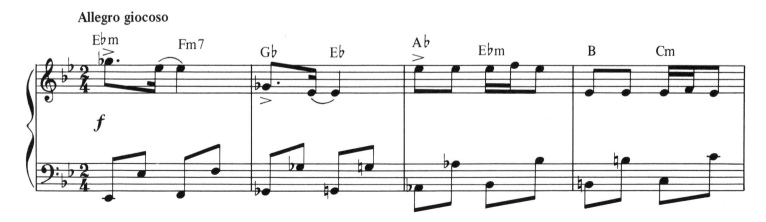

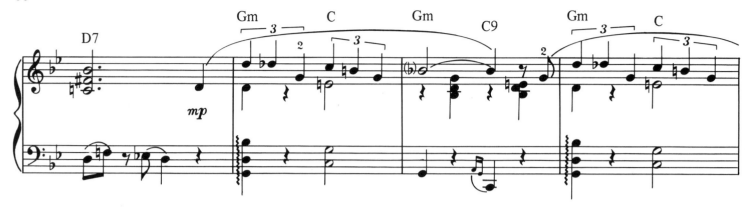

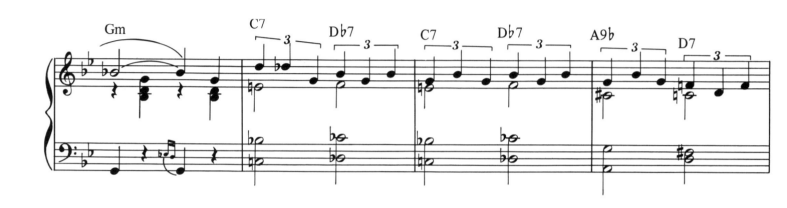

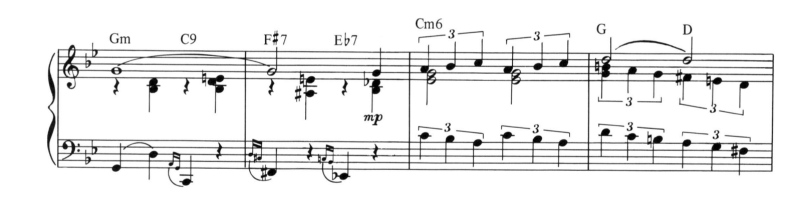

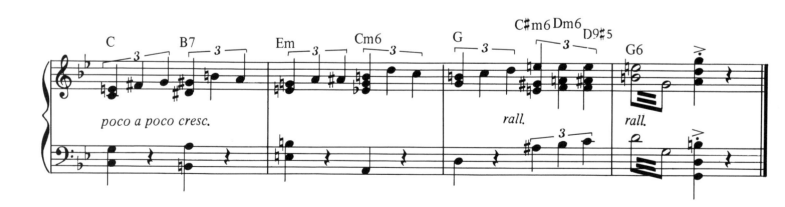

Bess You Is My Woman

from Porgy and Bess *(1935)*

**Words & Music by George Gershwin,
DuBose & Dorothy Heyward & Ira Gershwin**

Andantino cantabile

Summertime
from Porgy and Bess (1935)

**By George Gershwin, Ira Gershwin,
DuBose & Dorothy Heyward**

They Can't Take That Away From Me

from Shall We Dance *(1937)*

**Music & Lyrics by George Gershwin
& Ira Gershwin**

Moderate bounce

Themes *from* Rhapsody in Blue
(1924)

By George Gershwin
Arrangement based on the orchestration by Ferde Grofe

Moderato

Themes *from* Concerto in F
(1925)

Andante sostenuto (♩ = **104**)

By George Gershwin

Allegretto (♩ = 88)

Moderato con moto

espr. *mf*

Themes *from* An American in Paris
(1928)

By George Gershwin

Allegretto

Moderately slow

Three Preludes for Piano
1.

By George Gershwin

2.

3.

Allegro ben ritmato e deciso (♩ = 116)

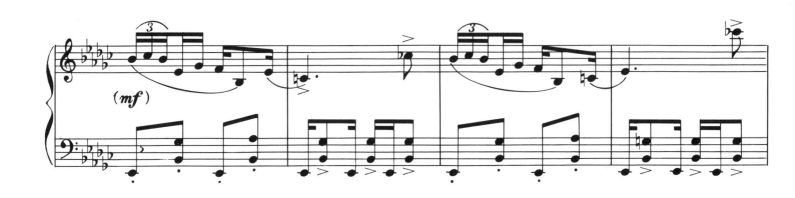

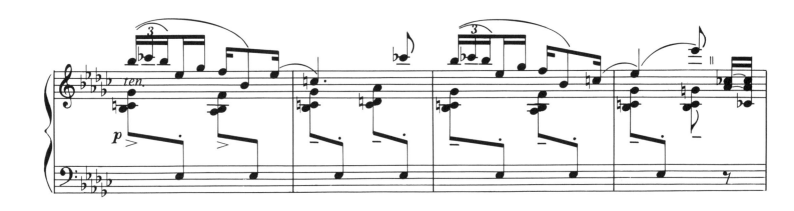

64